D1580467

8/2173500

Red is the Rose

A BOOK OF IRISH LOVE POEMS

First published 2011 by The O'Brien Press Ltd,
12 Terenure Road East, Rathgar, Dublin 6, Ireland.
Tel: +353 1 4923333; Fax: +353 1 4922777
E-mail: books@obrien.ie
Website: www.obrien.ie

ISBN: 978-1-84717-236-5
Copyright for text as a collection,
and for layout and design © The O'Brien Press, 2010
Copyright for photographs © Jonathan Rossney

A catalogue record for this title is available from the British Library.

1 2 3 4 5 6 7 8 9 10
11 12 13 14 15 16
Printed and bound in Poland by Białostockie Zakłady Graficzne S.A.
The paper used in this book is produced using pulp from managed forests.

Red is the Rose

A BOOK OF IRISH LOVE POEMS

THE O'BRIEN PRESS
DUBLIN

Contents

'INVENTIONS OF DELIGHT'

The Time I've Lost in Wooing

The time I've lost in wooing,
In watching and pursuing
The light that lies
In woman's eyes,
Has been my heart's undoing.
Though Wisdom oft has sought me,
I scorn'd the lore she brought me,
My only books
Were woman's looks,
And folly's all they've taught me.

Her smile when Beauty granted,
I hung with gaze enchanted,
Like him the Sprite,
Whom maids by night
Oft meet in glen that's haunted.
Like him, too, Beauty won me,
But while her eyes were on me,
If once their ray
Was turn'd away,
O! winds could not outrun me.

And are those follies going?

And is my proud heart growing

Too cold or wise

For brilliant eyes

Again to set it glowing?

No, vain, alas! the endeavour

From bonds so sweet to sever;

Poor Wisdom's chance

Against a glance

Is now as weak as ever.

Thomas Moore

A Poet To His Beloved

I bring you with reverent hands
The books of my numberless dreams,
White woman that passion has worn
As the tide wears the dove-grey sands,
And with heart more old than the horn
That is brimmed from the pale fire of time:
White woman with numberless dreams,
I bring you my passionate rhyme.

W.B. Yeats

The Snowy-Breasted Pearl

There's a colleen fair as May,
For a year and for a day
I've sought by every way her heart to gain.
There's no art of tongue or eye
Fond youths with maidens try
But I've tried with ceaseless sigh, yet tried in vain.
If to France or far-off Spain
She'd cross the watery main,
To see her face again the sea I'd brave.
And if 'tis heaven's decree
That mine she may not be
May the son of Mary me in mercy save!

O thou blooming milk-white dove,
To whom I've given true love,
Do not ever thus reprove my constancy.
There are maidens would be mine,
With wealth in hand and kine,
If my heart would but incline to turn from thee.
But a kiss with welcome bland,
And a touch of thy dear hand,
Are all that I demand, would'st thou not spurn;
For if not mine, dear girl,
O Snowy-Breasted Pearl!
May I never from the fair with life return!

Translated by Sir George Petrie

He Wishes for the Cloths of Heaven

Had I the heavens' embroidered cloths,
Enwrought with golden and silver light,
The blue and the dim and the dark cloths
Of night and light and the half-light,
I would spread the cloths under your feet:
But I, being poor, have only my dreams;
I have spread my dreams under your feet;
Tread softly because you tread on my dreams.

W.B. Yeats

The Lark In The Clear Air

Dear thoughts are in my mind, and my soul soars enchanted,
As I hear the sweet lark sing, in the clear air of the day,
For a tender beaming smile to my hope has been granted,
And tomorrow she shall hear all my fond heart would say.

I shall tell her all my love, all my soul's adoration.
And I think she will hear me, and will not say me nay;
It is this that gives my soul all its joyous elation,
As I hear the sweet lark sing, in the clear air of the day.

Traditional

Is It a Month

Is it a month since I and you
In the starlight of Glen Dubh
Stretched beneath a hazel bough
Kissed from ear and throat to brow,
Since your fingers, neck, and chin
Made the bars that fenced me in,
Till Paradise seemed but a wreck
Near your bosom, brow, and neck,
And stars grew wilder, growing wise,
In the splendour of your eyes!
Since the weasel wandered near
Whilst we kissed from ear to ear
And the wet and withered leaves
Blew about your cap and sleeves,
Till the moon sank tired through the ledge
Of the wet and windy hedge?
And we took the starry lane
Back to Dublin town again.

J. M. Synge

New Love

The day I knew you loved me we had lain
Deep in Coill Doraca down by Gleann na Scath
Unknown to each till suddenly I saw
You in the Shadow, knew oppressive pain
Stopping my heart, and there you did remain
In dreadful beauty fair without a flaw,
Blinding the eyes that yet could not withdraw
Till wild between us drove the wind and rain.

Breathless we reached the brugh before the west
Burst in full fury – then with lightning stroke
The tempest in my heart roared up and broke
Its barriers, and I swore I would not rest
Till that mad heart was worthy of your breast
Or dead for you – and then this love awoke.

Joseph Mary Plunkett

The Kiss

Give me, my love, that billing kiss
I taught you one delicious night,
When, turning epicures in bliss,
We tried inventions of delight.

Come, gently steal my lips along,
And let your lips in murmurs move –
Ah, no! – again – that kiss was wrong –
How can you be so dull, my love?

'Cease, cease!' the blushing girl replied –
And in her milky arms she caught me –
'How can you thus your pupil chide;
You know 'twas in the dark you taught me!'

Thomas Moore

Love's Young Dream

Oh! the days are gone, when Beauty bright
My heart's chain wove;
When my dream of life, from morn till night,
Was love, still love.
New hope may bloom,
And days may come,
Of milder calmer beam,
But there's nothing half so sweet in life
As love's young dream:
No, there's nothing half so sweet in life
As love's young dream.

Though the bard to purer fame may soar,
When wild youth's past;
Though he win the wise, who frown'd before,
To smile at last;
He'll never meet
A joy so sweet,
In all his noon of fame,
As when first he sung to woman's ear
His soul-felt flame,
And, at every close, she blush'd to hear
The one loved name.

No, — that hallow'd form is ne'er forgot
Which first love traced;
Still it lingering haunts the greenest spot
On memory's waste.
'Twas odour fled
As soon as shed;
'Twas morning's winged dream;
'Twas a light, that ne'er can shine again
On life's dull stream:
Oh! 'twas light that n'er can shine again
On life's dull stream.

Thomas Moore

Brown Penny

I whispered, 'I am too young,'
And then, 'I am old enough';
Wherefore I threw a penny
To find out if I might love.
'Go and love, go and love, young man,
If the lady be young and fair.'
Ah, penny, brown penny, brown penny,
I am looped in the loops of her hair.

O love is the crooked thing,
There is nobody wise enough
To find out all that is in it,
For he would be thinking of love
Till the stars had run away
And the shadows eaten the moon.
Ah, penny, brown penny, brown penny,
One cannot begin it too soon.

W.B. Yeats

Pulse of My Heart

As the sweet blackberry's modest bloom,
Fair flowering, greets the sight,
Or strawberries, in their rich perfume,
Fragrance and bloom unite:
So this fair plant of tender youth
In outward charms can vie,
And from within the soul of truth,
Soft beaming fills her eye.
Pulse of my heart! Dear source of care,
Stolen sighs, and love-breathed vows!
Sweeter than when through scented air
Gay bloom the apple boughs!
With thee no day can winter seem,
Nor frost nor blast can chill;
Thou the soft breeze, the cheering team,
That keeps it summer still.

Anonymous

21

REMEMBERED LOVE

And Then No More

I saw her once, one little while, and then no more:
'Twas Eden's light on Earth awhile, and then no more.
Amid the throng she passed along the meadow-floor:
Spring seemed to smile on Earth awhile, and then no more;
But whence she came, which way she went, what garb she wore
I noted not; I gazed awhile, and then no more!

I saw her once, one little while, and then no more!
'Twas Paradise on Earth awhile, and then no more.
Ah! what avail my vigils pale, my magic lore?
She shone before mine eyes awhile, and then no more.
The shallop of my peace is wrecked on Beauty's shore.
Near Hope's fair isle it rode awhile, and then no more!

I saw her once, one little while, and then no more:
Earth looked like Heaven a little while, and then no more.
Her presence thrilled and lighted to its inner core
My desert breast a little while, and then no more.
So may, perchance, a meteor glance at midnight o'er
Some ruined pile a little while, and then no more!

I saw her once, one little while, and then no more:
The earth was Peri-land awhile, and then no more.
Oh, might I see but once again, as once before,
Through chance or wile, that shape awhile,
                    and then no more!
Death soon would heal my griefs! This heart,
                    now sad and sore,
Would beat anew a little while, and then no more.

James Clarence Mangan

The Song of Wandering Aengus

I went out to the hazel wood,
Because a fire was in my head,
And cut and peeled a hazel wand,
And hooked a berry to a thread;
And when white moths were on the wing,
And moth-like stars were flickering out,
I dropped the berry in a stream
And caught a little silver trout.

When I had laid it on the floor
I went to blow the fire aflame,
But something rustled on the floor,
And some one called me by my name:
It had become a glimmering girl
With apple blossom in her hair
Who called me by my name and ran
And faded through the brightening air.

Though I am old with wandering
Through hollow lands and hilly lands,
I will find out where she has gone,
And kiss her lips and take her hands;
And walk among long dappled grass,
And pluck till time and times are done
The silver apples of the moon,
The golden apples of the sun.

W.B. Yeats

We Parted in Silence

We parted in silence, we parted by night,
On the banks of that lonely river;
Where the fragrant limes their boughs unite,
We met – and we parted forever!
The night-bird sung, and the stars above
Told many a touching story,
Of friends long passed to the kingdom of love,
Where the soul wears its mantle of glory.
We parted in silence – our cheeks were wet
With the tears that were past controlling;
We vowed we would never, no, never forget,
And those vows at the time were consoling;
But those lips that echoed the sounds of mine
Are as cold as that lonely river;
And that eye, that beautiful spirit's shrine,
Has shrouded its fires forever.
And now on the midnight sky I look,
And my heart grows full of weeping;
Each star is to me a sealéd book,
Some tale of that loved one keeping.
We parted in silence – we parted in tears,
On the banks of that lonely river:
But the odour and bloom of those bygone years
Still hang o'er its waters forever.

Isabella Valancy Crawford

He Tells Of A Valley Full Of Lovers

I dreamed that I stood in a valley, and amid sighs,
For happy lovers passed two by two where I stood;
And I dreamed my lost love came stealthily out of the wood
With her cloud-pale eyelids falling on dream-dimmed eyes:
I cried in my dream, O women, bid the young men lay
Their heads on your knees, and drown their eyes with your fair,
Or remembering hers they will find no other face fair
Till all the valleys of the world have been withered away.

W.B. Yeats

To Helene

I sent a ring — a little band
Of emerald and ruby stone,
And bade it, sparkling on thy hand,
Tell thee sweet tales of one
Whose constant memory
Was full of loveliness, and thee.

A shell was graven on its gold, —
'Twas Cupid fix'd without his wings —
To Helene once it would have told
More than was ever told by rings:
But now all's past and gone,
Her love is buried with that stone.

Thou shalt not see the tears that start
From eyes by thoughts like these beguiled;
Thou shalt not know the beating heart,
Ever a victim and a child:
Yet Helene, love, believe
The heart that never could deceive.

I'll hear thy voice of melody
In the sweet whispers of the air;
I'll see the brightness of thine eye
In the blue evening's dewy star;
In crystal streams thy purity;
And look on Heaven to look on thee.

George Darley

Do You Remember That Night?

Do you remember that night
That you were at the window,
With neither hat nor gloves,
Nor coat to shelter you;
I reached out my hand to you,
And you ardently grasped it,
And I remained in converse with you
Until the lark began to sing?

Do you remember that night
That you and I were
At the foot of the rowan tree,
And the night drifting snow;
Your head on my breast,
And your pipe sweetly playing?
I little thought that night
Our ties of love would ever loosen.

O beloved of my inmost heart,
Come some night, and soon,
When my people are at rest,
That we may talk together;
My arms shall encircle you,
While I relate my sad tale
That it is your pleasant, soft converse
That has deprived me of heaven.
The fire is unraked,
The light extinguished,
The key under the door,
And do you softly draw it.
My mother is asleep,
And I am quite awake;
My fortune is in my hand,
And I am ready to go with you.

Translated by Eugene O'Curry

Inamorata

The bees were holding levees in the flowers,
Do you remember how each puff of wind
Made every wing a hum? My hand in yours
Was listening to your heart, but now
The glory is all faded, and I find
No more the olden mystery of the hours
When you were lovely and our hearts would bow
Each to the will of each, but one bright day
Is stretching like an isthmus in a bay
From the glad years that I have left behind.

I look across the edge of things that were
And you are lovely in the April ways,
Holy and mute, the sigh of my despair …
I hear once more the linnets' April tune
Beyond the rainbow's warp, as in the days
You brought me facefuls of your smiles to share
Some of your new-found wonders … Oh when soon
I'm wandering the wide seas for other lands,
Sometimes remember me with folded hands,
And keep me happy in your pious prayer.

Francis Ledwidge

When You are Old

When you are old and grey and full of sleep,
And nodding by the fire, take down this book,
And slowly read, and dream of the soft look
Your eyes had once, and of their shadows deep;

How many loved your moments of glad grace,
And loved your beauty with love false or true,
But one man loved the pilgrim soul in you,
And loved the sorrows of your changing face;

And bending down beside the glowing bars,
Murmur, a little sadly, how Love fled
And paced upon the mountains overhead
And hid his face amid a crowd of stars.

W.B. Yeats

35

'NO ONE HAS EVER LOVED BUT YOU AND I ...

Nocturne

The long day was bright,
It slowly passed from the purple slopes of the hill;
And then the night
Came floating quietly down, and the world grew still.
Now I lie awake,
The south wind stirs the white curtains to and fro.
Cries the corncrake
In fields that stretch by the stream-side, misty and low.
At the meadow's edge
I know the faint pink clover is heavy with dew.
Under the hedge
The speedwell closes its sweet eyes, dreamily blue.
With pursed rosy lips
The baby buds are asleep on the apple tree.
The river slips
Beneath the scarcely swayed willows, on to the sea.
The dark grows, and grows,
But I'm too happy to sleep, and the reason why
No creature knows,
Save certain little brown birds, and my love, and I.

Frances Wynne

Oh, Call It by Some Better Name

Oh, call it by some better name,
For Friendship sounds too cold,
While Love is now a worldly flame,
Whose shrine must be of gold;
And Passion, like the sun at noon,
That burns o'er all he sees,
Awhile as warm, will set as soon –
Then, call it none of these.
Imagine something purer far,
More free from stain of clay
Than Friendship, Love or Passion are,
Yet human still as they:
And if thy lip, for love like this,
No mortal word can frame,
Go, ask of angels what it is,
And call it by that name.

Thomas Moore

My Hope, My Love

My hope, my love, we will go
Into the woods, scattering the dews,
Where we will behold the salmon, and the ousel in its nest,
The deer and the roe-buck calling,
The sweetest bird on the branches warbling,
The cuckoo on the summit of the green hill;
And death shall never approach us
In the bosom of the fragrant wood!

Anonymous

Queens

Seven dog-days we let pass
Naming Queens in Glenmacnass,
All the rare and royal names
Wormy sheepskin yet retains,
Etain, Helen, Maeve, and Fand,
Golden Deirdre's tender hand,
Bert, the big-foot, sung by Villon,
Cassandra, Ronsard found in Lyon.
Queens of Sheba, Meath and Connaught,
Coifed with crown, or gaudy bonnet,
Queens whose finger once did stir men,
Queens were eaten of fleas and vermin,
Queens men drew like Mona Lisa,
Or slew with drugs in Rome and Pisa,
We named Lucrezia Crivelli,
And Titian's lady with amber belly,
Queens acquainted in learned sin,
Jane of Jewry's slender shin:
Queens who cut the bogs of Glanna,
Judith of Scripture, and Gloriana,
Queens who wasted the East by proxy,
Or drove the ass-cart, a tinker's doxy,
Yet these are rotten – I ask their pardon –
And we've the sun on rock and garden,
These are rotten, so you're the Queen
Of all the living, or have been.

J. M. Synge

Amo, Amas

Amo, Amas, I love a lass
As a cedar tall and slender;
Sweet cowslip's grace is her nominative case,
And she's of the feminine gender.
Rorum, Corum, sunt divorum,
Harum, Scarum divo;
Tag-rag, merry-derry, periwig and hat-band
Hic hoc horum genitivo.
Can I decline a Nymph divine?
Her voice as a flute is dulcis.
Her oculus bright, her manus white,
And soft, when I tacto, her pulse is.
Rorum, Corum, sunt divorum,
Harum, Scarum divo;
Tag-rag, merry-derry, periwig and hat-band
Hic hoc horum genitivo.
Oh, how bella my puella,
I'll kiss secula seculorum.
If I've luck, sir, she's my uxor,
O dies benedictorum.
Rorum, Corum, sunt divorum,
Harum, Scarum divo;
Tag-rag, merry-derry, periwig and hat-band
Hic hoc horum genitivo.

John O'Keefe

The Ragged Wood

O hurry where by water among the trees
The delicate-stepping stag and his lady sigh,
When they have but looked upon their images —
Would none had ever loved but you and I!

Or have you heard that sliding silver-shoed
Pale silver-proud queen-woman of the sky,
When the sun looked out of his golden hood? —
O that none ever loved but you and I!

O hurry to the ragged wood, for there
I will drive all those lovers out and cry —
O my share of the world, O yellow hair!
No one has ever loved but you and I.

W.B. Yeats

43

Had I a Golden Pound

Had I a golden pound to spend,
My love should mend and sew no more.
And I would buy her a little quern,
Easy to turn at the kitchen floor
And for her wondrous curtains white,
With birds in flight and flowers in bloom,
To face with pride the road to town,
And mellow down her sunlit room
And with the silver change we'd prove
The truth of Love to life's own end,
With hearts the year could but embolden,
Had I a golden pound to spend.

Francis Ledwidge

If Thou'lt Be Mine

If thou'lt be mine, the treasures of air,
Of earth, and sea, shall lie at thy feet;
Whatever in Fancy's eye looks fair,
Or in Hope's sweet music sounds most sweet,
Shall be ours – if thou wilt be mine, love!

Bright flowers shall bloom wherever we rove,
A voice divine shall talk in each stream;
The stars shall look like world of love,
And this earth be all one beautiful dream
In our eyes – if thou wilt be mine, love!

And thoughts, whose source is hidden and high,
Like streams that come from heaven-ward hills,
Shall keep our hearts, like meads, that lie
To be bathed by those eternal rills,
Ever green, if thou wilt be mine, love!

All this and more the Spirit of Love
Can breathe o'er them who feel his spells;
That heaven, which forms his home above,
He can make on earth, wherever he dwells,
As thou'lt own, – if thou wilt be mine, love!

Thomas Moore

The Heart Of The Woman

O what to me the little room
That was brimmed up with prayer and rest;
He bade me out into the gloom,
And my breast lies upon his breast.

O what to me my mother's care,
The house where I was safe and warm;
The shadowy blossom of my hair
Will hide us from the bitter storm.

O hiding hair and dewy eyes,
I am no more with life and death,
My heart upon his warm heart lies,
My breath is mixed into his breath.

W.B. Yeats

Song

Nothing but sweet music wakes
My Beloved, my Beloved.
Sleeping by the blue lakes,
My own Beloved!

Song of lark and song of thrush,
My Beloved! my Beloved!
Sing in morning's rosy bush,
My own Beloved!

When your eyes dawn blue and clear,
My Beloved! my Beloved!
You will find me waiting here,
My own Beloved!

Francis Ledwidge

ROMANCING 'ROUND IRELAND

Youghal Harbour

One Sunday morning, into Youghal walking,
I met a maiden upon the way;
Her little mouth sweet as fairy music,
Her soft cheek blushing like dawn of day!
I laid a bold hand upon her bosom,
And asked a kiss: but she answered: 'No:
Fair sir, be gentle; do not tear my mantle;
'Tis none in Erin my grief can know.

'Tis but a little hour since I left Youghal,
And my love forbade me to return;
And now my weary way I wander
Into Cappoquin, a poor girl forlorn:
Then do not tempt me; for, alas, I dread them
Who with tempting proffers teach girls to roam
Who'd first deceive us, then faithless leave us,
And send us shame-faced and bare-foot home.'

'My heart and hand here! I mean you marriage!
I have loved like you and known love's pain;
And if you turn back now to Youghal Harbour,
You ne'er shall want house or home again:
You shall have a lace cap like any lady,
Cloak and capuchin, too, to keep you warm,
And if God pleases, maybe, a little baby,
By and by, to nestle within your arm.'

Anonymous

My Lagan Love

Where Lagan stream sings lullaby,
There blows a lily fair,
The twilight gleam is in her eye,
The night is on her hair.
And – like a love-sick lenanshee,
She hath my heart in thrall.
Nor life I owe, nor liberty,
For love is lord of all.

And often when the beetle's horn
Hath lulled her eye to sleep,
I steal unto her shieling lorn
And thro' the dooring peep;
There on the cricket's singing stone
She stirs the bog-wood fire,
And hums in sad, sweet undertone
The song of heart's desire.

Her welcome like her love for me
Is from the heart within.
Her warm kiss is felicity
That knows no taint or sin.
When she was only fairy small,
Her gentle mother died.
But true love keeps her memory warm
By Lagan's silver side.

Traditional

On Deborah Perkins of the County of Wicklow

Some sing ye of Venus the goddess

Some chant ye of rills, and of fountains;

But the theme of such praise,

As my fancy can raise,

Is a wench of the Wicklow mountains.

Mount Ida they surely surpass,

With the Wood-nymphs recess, and their lurkings;

O! 'tis there that I play

And wanton all day,

With little black Deborah Perkins.

King Solomon, he had nine hundred, at least,

To humour his taste, with their smirkings;

But not one of 'em all,

When she led up a ball,

Could foot it like Deborah Perkins.

The fair Cleopatra, Anthony loved,

But, by heaven, I'd give him his jerkings;

If that he was here,

And shou'd think to compare

That trollop, with Deborah Perkins.

Bacchus he prized Ariadne the sweet,

But I wish we were now at the firkins;

I'd make him reel off,

In contemptible scoff,

While I toasted plump Deborah Perkins.
Might I have all the girls at command,
That boast of their Dresden, or markings;
I'd rather feed goats,
And play with the coats
Of cherry-cheeked Deborah Perkins.
A fig for the eclogues of Maro,
Or Ovid's fantastical workings;
If I haven't their letters,
I sing of their betters,
When I touch up young Deborah Perkins.

Anonymous

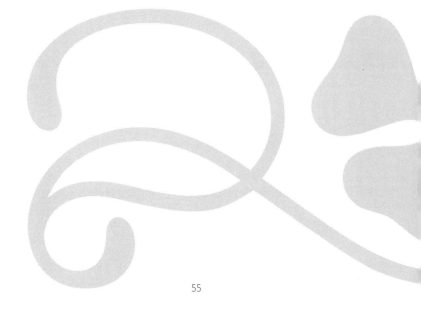

The Lapful of Nuts

Whene'er I see soft hazel eyes
And nut-brown curls,
I think of those bright days I spent
Among the Limerick girls;
When up through Cratla woods I went,
Nutting with thee;
And we plucked the glossy clustering fruit
From many a bending tree.

Beneath the hazel boughs we sat,
Thou, love, and I,
And the gathered nuts lay in thy lap,
Beneath thy downcast eye:
But little we thought of the store we'd won,
I, love, or thou;
For our hearts were full, and we dare not own
The love that's spoken now.
Oh, there's wars for willing hearts in Spain,
And high Germanie!
And I'll come back, 'ere long, again,
With knightly fame and fee:
And I'll come back, if I ever come back,
Faithful to thee,
That sat with thy white lap full of nuts
Beneath the hazel tree.

Anonymous

Lovely Mary Donnelly

Oh, lovely Mary Donnelly, my joy, my only best
If fifty girls were round you, I'd hardly see the rest;
Be what it may the time o' day, the place be where it will
Sweet looks o' Mary Donnelly, they bloom before me still.

Her eyes like mountain water that's flowing on a rock,
How clear they are, how dark they are! they give me many a shock.
Red rowans warm in sunshine and wetted with a shower,
Could ne'er express the charming lip that has me in its power.

Her nose is straight and handsome, her eyebrows lifted up,
Her chin is very neat and pert, and smooth like a china cup,
Her hair's the brag of Ireland, so weighty and so fine;
It's rolling down upon her neck, and gathered in a twine.

The dance o' last Whit-Monday night exceeded all before,
No pretty girl from miles about was missing from the floor,
But Mary kept the belt of love, and O but she was gay!
She danced a jig, she sung a song, that took my heart away.

When she stood up for dancing, her steps were so complete,
The music nearly killed itself to her feet;
The fiddler mourned his blindness, he heard her so much praised,
But blessed his luck not to be deaf when once her voice she raised.

And evermore I'm whistling or lilting what you sung,
Your smile is always in my heart, your name beside my tongue;
But you've as many sweethearts as you'd count on both your hands,
And for myself there's not a thumb or little finger stands.

Oh, you're the flower o' womankind in country or in town;
The higher I exalt you, the lower I'm cast down.
If some great lord should come this way, and see your beauty bright
And you to be his lady, I'd own it was but right.

Oh, might we live together in a lofty palace hall,
Where joyful music rises, and where scarlet curtains fall!
With sods or grass the only roof, and mud the only wall!

O lovely Mary Donnelly, your beauty's my distress,
It's far too beauteous to be mine, but I'll never wish it less.
The proudest place would fit your face, and I am poor and low
But blessings be about you, dear, wherever you may go.

William Allingham

'WHO COULD DENY YOU LOVE?'

It Is Not Beauty I Demand

It is not Beauty I demand,
A crystal brow, the moon's despair,
Nor the snow's daughter, a white hand,
Nor mermaid's yellow pride of hair.

Tell me not of your starry eyes,
Your lips that seem on roses fed,
Your breasts where Cupid trembling lies,
Nor sleeps for kissing of his bed.

A bloomy pair of vermeil cheeks,
Like Hebe's in her ruddiest hours,
A breath that softer music speaks
Than summer winds a-wooing flowers.

These are but gauds; nay, what are lips?
Coral beneath the ocean-stream,
Whose brink when your adventurer sips
Full oft he perisheth on them.

And what are cheeks but ensigns oft
That wave hot youth to fields of blood?
Did Helen's breast though ne'er so soft,
Do Greece or Ilium any good?

Eyes can with baleful ardour burn,
Poison can breath that erst perfumed,
There's many a white hand holds an urn
With lovers' hearts to dust consumed.

For crystal brows — there's naught within,
They are but empty cells for pride;
He who the Syren's hair would win
Is mostly strangled in the tide.

Give me, instead of beauty's bust,
A tender heart, a loyal mind,
Which with temptation I could trust,
Yet never linked with error find.

One in whose gentle bosom I
Could pour my secret heart of woes.
Like the care-burdened honey-fly
That hides his murmurs in the rose.

My earthly comforter! whose love
So indefeasible might be,
That when my spirit won above
Hers could not stay for sympathy.

George Darley

Dear Dark Head

Put your head, darling, darling, darling,
Your darling black head my heart above;
Oh, mouth of honey, with the thyme for fragrance,
Who with heart in breast could deny you love?

Oh, many and many a young girl for me is pining,
Letting her locks of gold to the cold wind free,
For me, the foremost of our gay young fellows;
But I'd leave a hundred, pure love, for thee!

Then put your head, darling, darling, darling,
Your darling black head my heart above;
Oh, mouth of honey, with the thyme for fragrance,
Who, with heart in breast, could deny you love?

Translated by Sir Samuel Ferguson

Your Songs

If I have you then I have everything
In One, and that One nothing of them all
Nor all compounded, and within the wall
Beneath the tower I wait to hear you sing:
Love breathing low above the breast of Spring,
Pressing her heart with baby heart and small
From baby lips love-syllables lets fall
And strokes with gentle hand her quivering wing.

You come rejoicing all the wilderness,
Filling with praise the land to joy unknown,
Fresh from that garden whose perfumes have blown
Down through the valley of the cypresses —
O heart, you know not your own loveliness,
Nor these your songs, for they are yours alone.

Joseph Mary Plunkett

On Beauty

Beauty gilds the blushing morn,
Hangs the dew-drop on the thorn,
Paints the rose in richest bloom,
Fills the air with sweet perfume:
But sweet perfume,
Nor rose in bloom,
Nor dew-drop bright,
Nor morning light,
In charms can vie
With woman's eye.
In woman's eye we raptured view
Beauty at once, and pleasure too.

John Kelly

She

The white bloom of the blackthorn, she,
The small sweet raspberry-blossom, she;
More fair the shy, rare glance of her eye,
Than the wealth of the world to me.

My heart's pulse, my secret, she,
The flower of the fragrant apple, she;
A summer glow o'er the winter's snow,
'Twixt Christmas and Easter, she.

Anonymous

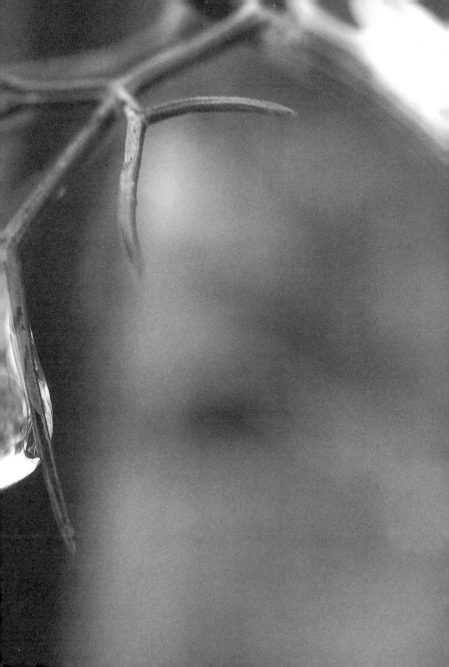

The Lions

Her hair's the canopy of heaven,
Her eyes the pools of healing are,
Her words wild prophecies whose seven
Thunders resound from star to star.

Her hands and feet are jewels fine
Wrought for the edifice of all grace,
Her breath inebriates like wine –
The blinding beauty of her face
Is lovelier than the primal light
And holds her lover's pride apart
To tame the lions of the night
That range the wilderness of his heart.

Joseph Mary Plunkett

The Vision of Love

The twilight fleeted away in pearl on the stream,
And night, like a diamond done, stood still in our dream.
Your eyes like burnished stones or as stars were bright
With the sudden vision that made us one with the night.

We loved in infinite spaces, forgetting here
The breasts that were lit with life and the lips so near;
Till the wizard willows waved in the wind and drew
Me away from the fullness of love and down to you.

Our love was so vast that it filled the heavens up:
But the soft white form I held was an empty cup,
When the willows called me back to earth with their sigh,
And we moved as shades through the deep that was you and I.

AE (George William Russell)

'LOVELY AND FAIR AS THE
ROSE OF THE SUMMER ...'

Red is the Rose

Red is the rose that in yonder garden grows
Fair is the lily of the valley
Clear is the water that flows from the Boyne
But my love is fairer than any.
Come over the hills, my bonnie Irish lass
Come over the hills to your darling
You choose the rose, love, and I'll make the vow
And I'll be your true love forever.

'Twas down by Killarney's green woods that we strayed
When the moon and the stars they were shining
The moon shone its rays on her locks of golden hair
And she swore she'd be my love forever.

It's not for the parting that my sister pains
It's not for the grief of my mother
'Tis all for the loss of my bonny Irish lass
That my heart is breaking forever.

Traditional

A White Rose

The red rose whispers of passion,
And the white rose breathes of love;
O, the red rose is a falcon,
And the white rose is a dove.

But I send you a cream-white rosebud
With a flush on its petal tips;
For the love that is purest and sweetest
Has a kiss of desire on the lips.

John Boyle O'Reilly

The Rose of Mooncoin

How sweet is to roam by the sunny Shure stream
And hear the doves coo 'neath the morning sunbeam
Where the thrush and the robin their sweet notes entwine
On the banks of the Shure that flows down by Mooncoin.
Flow on, lovely river, flow gently along
By your waters so sweet sounds the lark's merry song
On your green banks I wander where first I did join
With you, lovely Molly, the rose of Mooncoin.

Oh Molly, dear Molly, it breaks my fond heart
To know that we two forever must part
I'll think of you Molly while sun and moon shine
On the banks of the Shure that flows down by Mooncoin.

Then here's to the Shure with its valley so fair
As oftimes we wandered in the cool morning air
Where the roses are blooming and lilies entwine
On the banks of the Shure that flows down by Mooncoin.

Flow on, lovely river, flow gently along
By your waters so sweet sounds the lark's merry song
On your green banks I wander where first I did join
With you, lovely Molly, the rose of Mooncoin.

Watt Murphy

The Last Rose of Summer

'Tis the last rose of Summer,
Left blooming alone;
All her lovely companions
Are faded and gone;
No flower of her kindred,
No rose-bud is nigh,
To reflect back her blushes,
Or give sigh for sigh!

I'll not leave thee, thou lone one,
To pine on the stem;
Since the lovely are sleeping,
Go sleep thou with them.
Thus kindly I scatter
Thy leaves o'er the bed
Where thy mates of the garden
Lie scentless and dead.

So soon may I follow,
When friendships decay,
And from Love's shining circle
The gems drop away!
When true hearts lie wither'd,
And fond ones are flown,
Oh! who would inhabit
This bleak world alone?

Thomas Moore

The Little Black Rose Shall Be Red At Last

Because we share our sorrows and our joys
And all your dear and intimate thoughts are mine
We shall not fear the trumpets and the noise
Of battle, for we know our dreams divine,
And when my heart is pillowed on your heart
And ebb and flowing of their passionate flood
Shall beat in concord love through every part
Of brain and body – when at last the blood
O'erleaps the final barrier to find
Only one source wherein to spend its strength
And we two lovers, long but one in mind
And soul, are made one only flesh at length;
Praise God if this my blood fulfils the doom
When you, dark rose, shall redden into bloom.

Joseph Mary Plunkett

'TIME WILL BUT MAKE THEE MORE DEAR ...'

Believe me, if all those endearing young charms

Believe me, if all those endearing young charms
Which I gaze on so fondly to-day,
Were to change by to-morrow and fleet in my arms,
Like fairy gifts fading away.
Thou wouldst still be adored as this moment thou art,
Let thy loveliness fade as it will,
And around the dear ruin each wish of my heart,
Would entwine itself verdantly still.

It is not while beauty and youth are thine own
And thy cheeks unprofaned by a tear,
That the fervour and faith of a soul can be known,
To which time will but make thee more dear:
No, the heart that has truly loved never forgets,
But as truly loves on to the close,
As the sun-flower turns on her god when he sets
The same look which she turn'd when he rose.

Thomas Moore

Any Wife

Nobody knows but you and I, my dear,
And the stars, the spies of God, that lean and peer,
Those nights when you and I in a narrow strait
Were under the ships of God and desolate.
In extreme pain, in uttermost agony,
We bore the cross for each other, you and I,
When, through the darkest hour, the night of dread,
I suffered and you supported my head.

Ties that bind us together for life and death,
O hard-set fight in the darkness, shuddering breath,
Because a man can only bear as he may,
And find no tears for easing, the woman's way,
Anguish of pity, sharp in the heart like a sword;
Dost Thou not know, O Lord? Thou knowest, Lord,
What we endured for each other: our wounds were red
When he suffered and I supported his head.

Grief that binds us closer than smile or kiss,
Into the pang God slips the exquisite bliss.
You were my angel and I your angel, as he,
The angel, comforted Christ in His agony,
Lifting Him up from the earth that His blood made wet,
Pillowing the Holy Head, dabbled in sweat,
Thou who wert under the scourges knowest to prove
Love by its pangs, love that endures for love.

Katharine Tynan

My Love is Like a Cabbage

My love is like a cabbage
That's easy cut in two.
The leaves I'll give to others
But the heart I'll keep for you.

Oral poem from Tyrone

The Folly of Being Comforted

One that is ever kind said yesterday:
'Your well-beloved's hair has threads of grey,
And little shadows come about her eyes;
Time can but make it easier to be wise
Though now it seems impossible, and so
All that you need is patience.'
Heart cries, 'No,
I have not a crumb of comfort, not a grain,
Time can but make her beauty over again:
Because of that great nobleness of hers
The fire that stirs about her, when she stirs,
Burns but more clearly. O she had not these ways
When all the wild summer was in her gaze.'

O heart! O heart! If she'd but turn her head,
You'd know the folly of being comforted.

W.B. Yeats

Index of titles

Index of first lines